If It Walks Like a Duck...

and Other Truths My Mother Taught Me

GWEN JIMMERE

r

Roberkin Press

If It Walks Like a Duck...
and Other Truths My Mother Taught Me

First Printing: March 2009. Roberkin Press, Cleveland, OH.

*Truth 6 originally published as book excerpt by author at CarrieandDanielle.com. Portions of Truth 7 originally published as book excerpt by author at TheDuckWalk.com.

ISBN-10#: 0-578-00176-4 | ISBN-13#: 978-0-578-00176-0

Publisher: Roberkin Press, a Twisted Pearl Media Group Company
Managing Editor: Jill R. Freedman
Supporting Editors: W.A. Gordon, Danielle Afton
Cover, Interior Book Design/Production: Lisa Peterson
Illustrations: Michael Meister
Photography & Makeup: MobiusCo Photo & Andrew Lundberg

Dedication

This book is dedicated to:

My mother, whose years of quirky quotes dipped in love and encased in experience have not been in vain.

The life and memory of Michael Jerome Carter, Jr. I miss you, Mike-Mike. Can't wait to see you again.

Acknowledgements

To my father in Heaven, without whom nothing would be possible and life for me would be without meaning…

To my mother, father, sister, and nephews for all their relentless support, undying love, and never-ending commitment to helping me chase my many rainbows…

To my phenomenally talented editing, design, and glam teams, for bringing their A-games to each of their respective positions, and for remaining steadfast and patient with me throughout each crazy question, ongoing revision, and last-minute decision…

To each and every one of my friends who refused to bring cups ☺, but ended up with slightly damp, tear-stained shoulders, chocolate wine-laced lunch breaks, sleepless nights, or high cell phone overage charges from listening to me ramble for hours on end...

To each friend, acquaintance, and colleague who has contributed their insights, thoughts, support, personal stories, expertise, and time...

THANK YOU!

Trademarks Acknowledgement

The author and publisher acknowledge the trademarked and copyrighted statuses, as well as the trademark and copyright owners of the following listed works mentioned in this book:

"Cheaper By the Dozen": Twentieth Century Fox Film Corp.

"He's Just Not That Into You": New Line Productions, Inc.

"How the Grinch Stole Christmas": Random House, Inc.

"I Knew I Loved You": Sony BMG

"Keep On Walkin'": A&M Records

Radio Flyer: Radio Flyer, Inc.

"The Choice is Yours": Island Def Jam Music Group

"The Price is Right": FreemantleMedia North America, Inc.

Contents

Preface

"Pain is love."

Practically all of America has seen the film adaptation of *He's Just Not That Into You* and the opening scene couldn't be more spot on. As little girls, we are often taught that when a boy pushes us off the swing during recess and wipes his boogers in our hair during snack time, it means he likes us. And don't let him steal our favorite blanket during nap time—that means he *really* digs us.

Innocent enough, sure...if you're into falling face first into the dirt and picking nose slime out of your flowing locks. But come on, we were just kids, right? Maybe so. However, these early lessons in romance lay the groundwork for many of the unfavorable behaviors we subconsciously learn to accept as we mature into women.

As adults, too many things we know should be intolerable become the very things we end up inadvertently condoning in our intimate relationships.

Well, I'm here to tell you that pain is, most definitely, not love. Love does not intentionally hurt, and those who love us certainly don't continue to do things they know will cause us pain—emotional or otherwise.

When it comes to intimate relationships, matters of the heart are nothing to sneeze at. And although the answer to the oft-asked question of what love is will continue to be sought, there is a very clear and concise definition:

Love is patient, love is kind. It is not envious or arrogant with pride. Love is never boastful, conceited, selfish, or rude. Love never thinks just of itself, nor is it quick to take offense. It keeps no records of wrongs and is not resentful. Love does not delight in wrongdoings but is always glad to side with the truth. It always protects, always trusts, always hopes, always perseveres.[1]

That's it. As you can see, there are no crazy and outlandish statements about love's philosophical conundrum or the mathematical love equation some dead guy from France developed during the 15th century. The definition of love simply is what it is. While seemingly uncomplicated, the bar has been set very high. When I consider the men in my life who have uttered those three coveted words so easily, I can only think of a fraction who actually measured up to what that definition says. I ask you to take that same brief survey and contemplate who in your past fit the profile and who didn't.

With that said, pain and suffering due to bad relationships is not a rite of passage anyone is "required" to

1 I Corinthians 13:4-7. Holy Bible, International Standard Version.

endure. That's where I come in to save the day, and preserve your sanity at the same time. No need to thank me; it's all in a day's work.

The advice you will find in these next chapters is not in any way intended to be a substitute for psychological counseling, but instead, is an intimate relationship and personal accountability philosophy based upon my own experiences, and the experiences of numerous women and men who participated in research activities for the purpose of helping others through this book.

This book is all about realization, then application. In order to be able to find and accept real love from another person, we have to be able to genuinely live with and love ourselves first. To help you with this, you will find five "Truths for Living", followed by four "Truths for Loving". At the end of each "Truth", you will find an "Action Plan" to apply to your life, thereby helping you become the best "you" that you can be—in both life and in love. (Toward the very end, you'll see four appendices collectively titled, "Get Your Mind Right". These additional resources are in place to further the self-esteem, self-love, and self-worth you will be working on as we go along.)

We don't always get what we want, but we will certainly get what we expect. We all *want* to be treated well by our partners. However, if we *expect* others to treat us like trash, we will settle for relationships where we are treated as such. If we *expect* others to treat us well, we will only enter into relationships with people who treat us accordingly.

I know. I've been there. My mother taught me self-respect and self-love from an early age. She had high expectations in regard to her interactions with my father. Through their example, I knew what was to be tolerated in intimate relationships and what was not acceptable. Which battles were worth fighting and which ones weren't worth the energy. What behaviors were copacetic and which ones needed to be addressed.

As a teen, I, too, had high expectations of my boyfriends. If someone decided he wanted to cheat, I'd kiss him off instantly with a warning to not let the door hit him where the good Lord split him. Verbal, physical, and emotional abuse were absolute no-no's. I refused to be pressured for sex. And chivalry was definitely not dead. As a result, never once did I receive a broken heart, much less a wounded ego. Rarely did I have what one would call a "bad" relationship, and the only time I shed a tear over a guy was at the airport when I waved goodbye to my 12th grade boyfriend as he departed for military duty.

During and after college, I somehow developed a different set of expectations, a far cry from the tried and true ones learned from my parents. Bad relationships ended up becoming the norm. Emotional abuse was rampant and a broken heart seemed to be the status quo. I began to expect volatility in my relationships. Therefore, I settled for argumentative situations, controlling individuals, and disrespectful partners.

During one of these relationships, I cried so much and so often that I ended up with swollen tear ducts. Similarly, thousands of people are in awful situations and aren't fully aware of how detrimental these relationships are to their personal well-being. Even worse, millions have inner issues that must be dealt with before they can expect to enter into healthy, meaningful, long-term relationships. In order to fix the problems, we must first decide to explore where the roots of the problems lie. Only then can we repair them. As I've discovered, no one can be in a bad relationship unless they allow themselves to be in such a situation.

So, this book is for all the folks out

there who, for some reason or another, have yet to find out what true love of self, as well as true love from a partner, actually feels like. Those who are stuck in situations they have no idea how to get out of. People who are clueless as to how to even love at all. And last but not least, those who believe that pain is love.

I know that within each and every one of you lies the ability and desire to be an entirely beautiful person (or a **S.N.O.B.**, which I will explain later), inside and out. You have the drive and passion required to be independent and wise about the decisions you make for yourself—emotionally and otherwise.

It is my belief that we all simply need someone to help us focus on how to achieve this status every now and again, to let us know the many problems and pitfalls to be wary of, and to help us realize that we must acknowledge and address these issues when things are going awry so we can fix them.

Feel free to join in the conversation at:

www.TheDuckWalk.com

You can also email me directly at:

gwen@theduckwalk.com

Engage, absorb, and enlighten yourselves.

"You Stand Alone"

Truths for Living

Truth 1

"Beauty Doesn't Fade, Elasticity Does"

We women are like houses. Big, glamorous houses with serious curb appeal that inspire an entire neighborhood to upgrade their own backyards. Each of us are beautiful, gorgeous, fabulous, stunning, incredible, awe-inspiring, and just about every other compliment consisting of seven or more letters one can fathom. Unfortunately, just like that house with the amazing exterior, many of us have a few interior issues that could use a bit of handiwork to bring us up to code. Yes, it's the inside that counts, and although you've heard it all before, everyone knows how true this *cliché* is. Be that as it may, we truly have to attend to our inner selves before we can ever be entirely beautiful. So, what's your leaky faucet?

Of course, personal confidence in our outer beauty is essential, as well. Now, that doesn't give you a pass to shell out 20 grand just to get a "better" nose and an eyebrow lift. What it does mean is work with what you've got, girl! Okay, let's say you've got incredible eyes you love, but you're pretty sure your lips resemble something close to two pencil lines, which you've never been too thrilled about. Go ahead and enhance those optical beauties to their fullest potential (hey, if you've got it…flaunt it, right?), then maybe dab some simple lip balm or lip gloss on the kisser, bringing the most attention to those babies up top.

While this certainly is not a book on makeup tips, the men we love are indeed creatures of instant gratification. Allow me to clarify…

In the case of the typical man: if he isn't physically attracted to a particular woman when he first meets her, he's probably not going to see her as a first-class knockout six months later just because her charm is off the charts.

In the case of the typical woman: if she isn't physically attracted to a certain man when she first meets him, she might easily grow to love his looks, based upon how he treats her, based on *his* inner beauty. She once gagged at the thought of that animal pelt he calls back hair accidentally grazing her skin. Now, that *grotesque* disdain has been replaced by total adoration for the fur that keeps her warm at night. Gross? Perhaps, but as long as it makes her happy, it's all good.

Can't relate? No worries, I've got a better one for you. Late hip-hop star Notorious B.I.G. was an infamous ladies' man. With all due respect, attractiveness wasn't exactly his strong suit. I mean, even *he* called himself "ugly as ever".

Nevertheless, many of his women cited his charm, confidence, and charisma as what initially won them over. Trust me, it wasn't just his money and fame. Christopher Wallace had the ladies offering their legs up on a silver platter long before he ever donned the moniker "Biggie Smalls".

But really, who wants a "typical" man? As we continue, we'll discover how to attain the best *atypical* man for you. By the same token, who wants to be a "typical" woman? Each of us are unique and we want that individuality to shine, yes?

Put this one in your back pocket, chicas, 'cause this is going to change your life. You want to set yourself apart from the pack and effortlessly turn heads at the same time? Throw on a lil' confidence. Actually, a whole lot of confidence. Not to be misconstrued as arrogance, for that would be lame. I'm telling you, authentic confidence in herself, her looks, and her abilities is the sexiest, intangible thing a woman can have up her sleeve.

Ever met a blatantly unconfident man? Sometimes folks call them "soft". Yeah, that's not sexy at all. On the other hand, there are those meathead types who like to talk your head off and are way too brash for comfort. That's not hot, either. Conversely, a truly confident man is a chick-magnet. And for obvious reason. He doesn't need to brag and boast about his accomplishments or how big his wang is. His unspoken confidence and quiet strength speak volumes, and chicks dig it.

"Authentic confidence is the sexiest accessory"

Ditto for us ladies. I have acquaintances (who shall remain nameless just in case they're reading, but kudos for buying my book, girl!) who are not the best looking women walking the streets these days, yet they have more men fawning over them than the Tyra Banks and Heidi Klum lookalikes.

I could never understand this madness. How in the world were these women pulling the mirror images of Brad Pitt? There I was…definitely not a runway model, but I certainly knew I wasn't ugly…and I couldn't even pull the Hunchback of Notre Dame if I tried. I was well-educated, attractive, witty, and adventurous, yet incessantly single. For crying out loud, what was not to like?

Men can sense authentic confidence like a dog can sense fresh meat. (Did I just compare men to dogs? Sorry guys—Freudian slip… Just jokes, people, just jokes.) And no matter what my facial and physical features were or weren't, men were turned off by my pseudo-confidence. Many of my friends were getting married and starting families. Without realizing it, I was in "attack-mode", trying way too hard to get a man. Unbeknownst to me, my attitude was giving off a vibe of desperation that repelled, rather than attracted, the men I was interested in.

Likewise, some of the most beautiful women in the world are plagued with inner "self un-worthiness". What could these women possibly ever be unhappy about? Many are wealthy, gorgeous, sexy, powerful...did I mention wealthy? Yet, like my previous self, many have low-self esteem and may not even realize it. Others are insecure. Some are even suicidal and suffer from eating disorders. Just go to the grocery store, pick up a tabloid, and you'll find two or three poor-little-rich-things to gossip about by the water cooler tomorrow morning. Through my research, I found a common denominator to be that many of us, 1. didn't have a man in our lives or, 2. were in some pretty horrible relationships.

Let's say you're seriously depressed and you know in your heart that if you could only find a man to love you, all your problems would disappear. Wake up, sister! Do you realize how nutty that sounds? What is he going to do? Make like your fairy godfather and whisk all your troubles away with his magical electric shaver? Negative. After the initial "new man" euphoria wears down, you're going to be right back to having those same issues.

The fact is, your problems are not his problems. He can support you, drive you back and forth to the psychologist, and be the best thing in your life since the invention of the tampon. But, as my mother always says: "you stand alone". Even if he's your sole support system, he can't always empathize or sympathize at every moment. Whether he is with you or if you are by yourself, you and only you can make the changes needed to make yourself completely happy and entirely beautiful.

Allowing the possibility of marriage to validate me (an extension of poor self-esteem) was my leaky faucet. Yours could easily be something else.

No matter what fixer-upping you might require, you can handle it. The first step, of course, is self-admittance. Whether it's low confidence, poor self-esteem, depression, addiction, eating disorder(s), etc., you can make it happen for yourself. You *have* to make it happen for yourself. Continually engaging in problematical behavior displays a lack of love for oneself. You cannot fully love yourself if you know you have an issue and refuse to fix it to make yourself healthier. That is self-abuse and as entirely beautiful women, we are not going to abuse ourselves.

Furthermore, at some point, every woman has uttered the phrase, "He completes me". It sure does sound good. But remember, we get what we expect. Similarly, we speak what we expect into existence. If you expect *him* to complete you, how can you ever be complete for *yourself*? If he leaves you, are you to be incomplete once again? Instead, we need to aim for that same complete feeling, even before he arrives into the proverbial picture. You cannot, I repeat CANNOT, rely on your man—or anyone else, for that matter—to make you whole.

A complete and entirely beautiful woman will not tolerate many things we are going to explore in these next chapters. A complete woman will kick that dude to the curb in a millisecond if he is clowning around with her heart or in the relationship. She is a proud **S.N.O.B.** who **S**ettles for **N**othing **O**ther than the **B**est. She is complete enough and loves herself enough to expect *and* accept only what is best for her. Self-completion begins with self-love and with self-love comes the ability to make change within ourselves. (Fear not, my dear lovlies—we will revisit this guiding principle throughout the text.)

Self-love is one of the most important attributes we can have as women or, truth be told, as human beings. For one thing, if we had more self-love we wouldn't do things to our bodies that aren't cohesive with our well-being. And of course, we wouldn't enter into or stay in destructive relationships.

✦Your T1 Action Plan✦

For those who want help and don't know where to find it, you can get information about regional help centers, local to you, specializing in helping you be the best "you" that you can be, listed at:

http://mentalhealth.samhsa.gov/databases

Also, for a free self-esteem building help guide, visit:

http://mentalhealth.samhsa.gov/publications/allpubs/sma-3715/default.asp

Right on this website, you can find useful and practical things to do right now that can begin to help you on your journey toward self-completion and becoming entirely beautiful.

Need to hear a human voice? Gotcha covered. You can call the Substance Abuse and Mental Health Services Administration (SAMHSA) National Mental Health Information Center at:

1-800-789-2647

Let's start loving ourselves, and each other.

Truth 2

"Grown-Ups Don't Come With Manuals, Either"

Ah, the simplicities of childhood. Riding in your spanking, brand new Radio Flyer as Bobby from next door pulls you along. Playing hide-and-seek (or "hide-and-go-get-it", for you naughty girls) in the backyard. Chasing the ice cream truck down the street until it finally stops just for you. At an age where innocence and *naïveté* run rampant, no child or teen should have to endure the emotional pains that some know all too well. Unfortunately for children, sometimes they are more mature and better suited to be parents than the people who conceived them.

As we all know, the way in which we are reared during our formative years has an irrefutable effect on our adult lives. Regrettably, not everyone has the good fortune of having a stellar family life. Oftentimes, many of our mothers, fathers, or both, aren't around enough to even pay attention to us, let alone raise us. I believe we'd all agree: every child should ideally have two parents in the home. Of course that doesn't mean a single parent couldn't, and doesn't, do as good a job of rearing their child as two parents can.

But let's be honest. As kids, most of us want both our parents there with us each day. Let me tell you, though, just because mama or papa was a rolling stone doesn't mean you're alone.

Many people grow up with the same lingering anger they felt as children because one or both parents were not in their lives. It doesn't matter what the parents' reasoning was. The child, who has now grown into an adult, is still furious for feeling left and abandoned at such a young age, and rightfully so. But one day, we've got to forgive. If not for them, then definitely for our own well-being.

Easier said than done? Most definitely. But remember, you stand alone. If we continue to allow these bitter feelings to fester, the effects of an unhappy childhood will continue to exhibit themselves in the poor and destructive methods we use to cope. That's no good. So, rather than continuing to fume at the person(s) who inflicted such severe pain and disappointment, let's focus on clearing our minds of the tragedy faced while growing up. It's your world, and in this case, it's perfectly okay to feel it revolves around you.

During my research, I met a slew of amazing women whose parents were far from ideal. From what I have seen in many of these ladies, an estranged parent may haunt them forever and, in turn, cause these women to not trust the opposite sex for fear that this person will also abandon them. To quote my mother: "the root of the problem starts at home".

"The root of the problem starts at home"

It's true that the first man a girl learns to love is her father. If her father isn't present in her life or if he is disturbingly inattentive, this, sadly, may be an innocent child's first lesson in love. She may take that early experience to mean she should feel that men aren't committed, dedicated people, so why should she expect them to be? Her father certainly wasn't.

In the case of the child whose mother abandoned her or who constantly had different men around, she may grow up to be somewhat of a rolling stone herself, moving from man to man, never to be completely happy, and therefore rarely, if ever, feeling entirely beautiful.

While at a speaking engagement, I encountered an absolutely gorgeous young woman who grew up as a foster child and was "in the system" from birth until her late teens, when she was finally adopted. As a child, she was raised in an orphanage until she was sent to live with her first foster family, which resulted in the consequence of living under the tutelage of an incredibly cruel foster parent who, at times, beat her incessantly and pushed her down long flights of stairs. Thank God she was eventually transferred to a more loving, although very strict, home with suitable living arrangements. After a few more foster home transfers, she was eventually adopted by a great family that loves her unconditionally.

She made it explicitly clear that the constant change of environment, coupled with the horrid abuse she was victim to, has affected her personal life as an adult, as well as the success of her intimate relationships with men. Interestingly enough, she has a very young daughter and works incredibly hard to prevent the occurrence of a repeating cycle. She is quite proactive in ensuring her daughter will not succumb to ill-fated relationship woes due to seeing her mother's struggles, which have been directly influenced by the adversity endured during her childhood. In addition, she has taken large strides to continually develop her sense of self-worth by becoming an entirely beautiful **S.N.O.B.** What a phenomenal example for her daughter to emulate as she grows into womanhood!

In addition, many women have been subjected to molestation by relatives and family "friends". They have been raped or fondled at a young age, and then brainwashed by these sick adults, with the end result being that the victims have kept the abuse to themselves for fear of continued violation or retaliation.

If you can relate to any of this, please remember something. You are not unworthy of anything beautiful, just, or good. You did not deserve to be mistreated in *any* way. If this scenario resonates with you—if it's *about* you—I beg of you, please do not let some unsavory character from your past determine the happiness and prosperity of your future.

None of what happened was your fault. I completely understand how difficult it is to forgive those who have hurt us, but you must make it happen. Remember: you stand alone. Any and all animosity residing in your heart hinders YOU, and handicaps your personal growth and self-completion.

✦Your T2 Action Plan✦

Different people have different ways of handling their inner frustrations, disappointments, and anger. One of the most tried and true methods is writing it out. Write out everything you can about what happened, what didn't happen, and everything in between. But remember to avoid blaming yourself for the negligent, and perhaps abominable, behaviors of the adults in your childhood.

Get yourself a journal, a notebook, or a pad of paper. Consider starting up a blog if you are comfortable with the vulnerability that comes with allowing others to read your thoughts. Write every day or whenever the spirit moves you to do so. Vent your thoughts and your feelings about the occurrence(s), what the consequences seem to be, and how it still affects you.

Another method that often works, is

exercise. Go work out and sweat off some of that stress while clearing your mind. Physical activity and exercise are awesome ways to put a lot of aggression you may have built up for reasons that you know too well.

Lastly, consider making an appointment to visit a psychologist, psychiatrist, clinical social worker, or life coach. He or she can help you overcome the perils you are facing via their extensive expertise, skill, and training.

Note: Psychologists and psychiatrists often get a bad rap. Too many people out there have misconceptions about these professionals and believe you have to be "crazy" or clinically insane in order to visit a mental health professional. And if not, people are afraid that others will deem them as such. Allow me to reiterate: You...Stand...Alone. Always remember this. You are the one dealing with your concerns, no one else. YOU have to do what is necessary in order to better yourself. Tell the naysayers to kick rocks while you're passing by on your way to your psych appointment. It's time to get YOU together once and for all.

The truth is, it's often the healthiest people who visit psychologists, psychiatrists, clinical social workers, or life coaches. Very likely, effort is put forth by the people who know they can do better, who want to do what it takes to do better, and who are willing to put forth the effort to change their lives.

Truth 3

"A Good Hussy Makes Make Poor Housewife"

Did you know that, on average, people make assumptions about you within the first few seconds of planting their pupils on you? Amazing. They don't even know you, have barely had time to get your name, yet they have already decided if they dig your style or hate your guts. Even more surprising is that the vast majority of people will choose to say something *negative* about you rather than uttering anything positive. Think about it. Have you ever said, "I don't know, there's just something about Kristina I don't like"? But in reality, you really don't know anything about Kristina, other than she works at your job, wears way too much makeup (particularly those God-awful fake lashes), and can light a room with that cheap, overpowering perfume she wears *every* day. Who does she think she is anyway? Ugh!

No matter what her size, shape, or background, every woman wants to feel and be sexy. If she tells you otherwise, she's lying. And you can tell her I said so.

What's more, we ladies dress to impress. And we do a dang good job of it, don't we? We dress to impress ourselves, as well as those around us who we are most interested in. Let's not fool ourselves here, mamacitas. They don't keep designing the clothes to reveal more and more skin just because of the rise in global warming.

With that said, one must not only demand respect, we must also command it. We *demand* respect *after* getting to know whomever it is we want respect from. We *command* respect *before* they even get close enough to see the roots of our natural hair color. The commandment of respect is possessed in the way we walk, the way we talk, and even in the way we dress.

With the info we now know, it's reasonable to assume a guy will decide if he's attracted to a woman within the first few seconds of catching sight of her. How he talks to her initially may very well be determined by how she's dressed.

Let's assume you're at a party and you're getting your groove on alongside fifty of your closest friends. You spot some handsome stud locking eyes with one of the ladies in your vicinity of the venue.

Scenario 1

You see a young lady who has on a skirt that's not too short, but not too long, a cute tank top, and stiletto heels. You think she looks pretty hot, yet classy. So far, she's commanded the respect of the entire room without saying one word. She's mingling with her fellow socialites, laughing, dancing, and having a great time. He approaches her and respectfully compliments her (e.g., "You look great tonight."). They hold a brief conversation, he asks for her number, and she gives it to him. They go their separate ways and you don't see her go home with him that evening.

Scenario 2

You see a young lady who has on a barely-there miniskirt, a teeny, revealing halter top, and thigh-high stiletto boots. She hasn't commanded anyone's respect. It looks like she's possibly had a few too many and she's dancing as if she's being featured in a hip-hop video that should only air late at night when children should be asleep. He approaches her and instantly makes crude references to her body, then proceeds to smack her *derrière*. She now has two options: she can redeem herself by letting him know right then and there that his approach was totally unacceptable (you know, giving him that "I know you must have lost your mind" look and sternly stating, "Don't you ever touch me without my permission.") or she can offer up a flirty laugh. The first option might show him she demands to be respected and allow her to recoup a little of the respect she lost with that outfit. The other will give him an easy invitation to continue to grope and fondle her. She opts for the latter. Now he's feeling her up in the middle of the room and it appears she's totally into it. You see her leave the party with him, and you assume they're going to be knocking boots sometime before the night is over.

In *Scenario 1*, the young woman instantly earned (or it would be fair to say, "commanded") the respect she deserved without too much effort. She seemed to understand there is a vast difference between "sexy" and "slutty", and that one does not equate to the other. She was a lady, and the man who approached her apparently thought so, as well. He didn't fondle her or cross any boundaries. Certainly, he was attracted to her—that's why he approached her in the first place. After speaking with her, he asked her for her phone number, a request she obliged. He didn't assume she'd be going home with him that night. So, he gladly took the number and went on with his evening. She respected herself, and he was respectful to her in return. Of course, this is merely an example. Honestly, she could "get around" behind closed doors just as easily as anyone else. But based upon how she was dressed and how she acted, his initial impression of her isn't that he's automatically going to have a freaky Friday right off the bat, regardless of what may or may not actually happen.

On the other hand, it's not hard to

understand why most people would view the woman in *Scenario 2* objectionably. But the truth is, we don't know where she went with him that night. For all we know, he could have gone outside to walk her to her car (where her designated driver was waiting) and that's it. But because of the way she acted and how she was dressed, we've assumed he was about to "get lucky". She garnered no respect at all from anyone at the party, nor from the guy who approached her. Even if he didn't sleep with her that particular night, it's likely his impression is if he calls her a few times and maybe spends a couple bucks on a relatively cheap date, it'll be pretty simple for him to cinch an all-access panty pass. He saw what he figured was an easy target and went for the gusto.

When it comes to love, good guys don't want a promiscuous (or seemingly promiscuous) woman on their arms.

Presenting yourself as a lady is key. Now, that doesn't entail "doing as you're told", wearing long dresses, and minding your manners. This ain't the 50s. Being a lady is all about respecting yourself and is a direct derivative of self-love.

Below is a popular analogy you may have read or heard before. Please keep this in mind while on your journey toward becoming entirely beautiful:

Women are like apples on trees. The best ones are always at the top. Most men don't want to reach for the good ones because they are afraid of falling and getting hurt. Instead, these men simply grab the rotten apples with the bad seeds from the ground that aren't nearly as good, but are very easy to attain. The apples at the top are left to believe something is wrong with them, when in reality, they're the most amazing ones. They just have to wait for the right man to come along, the one who's brave enough to climb all the way to the top of the tree.

✦Your T3 Action Plan✦

You are one of those few apples at the top of the tree. Don't "dumb yourself down" in hopes of satisfying an ideal that you assume the cutie you've been eyeing will appreciate. Or because you believe the women who do that sort of thing are the ones who get all the guys. Besides, you don't want *all* the guys. Just the few that are willing to put forth the effort required to reach up high and grab you from the top.

To borrow a line from the popular 90s song, "you can get with this or you can get with that", but he should get with you, 'cause *you* are where it's at.

Truth 4

"Negativity is to Life as Dog Poo is to Shoes: Once You Step In It, It's Hard as Heck to Get Off"

Consider this: how much of the seven o'clock news is positive? Maybe two or three stories here and there about some sweet, little kid who rescued a stray bunny. But the vast majority of the news is negative. Murderers, thieves, rapists, and con artists are the stars. The father of five who works three jobs and is faithful to his wife, unfortunately, has no place on the news. Apparently, positive news doesn't draw the ratings. Who gives two hoots about that guy with the kids? Give us the latest celebrity love triangle any day. Catfight!

Now consider your friends, associates, and significant others. Know someone who rarely has anything positive to say? Someone who is always complaining, always gossiping, always trying to outdo others, always a "victim"? Those people are just like the vastly negative news. It's kind of depressing, don't you think?

I've discovered that most folks are quite interesting and pretty awesome. But I've also learned, very hard and very fast, that there are a few in this world who simply do not like to see other people's joy and will often resort to any means of bringing others down.

Many of these types run around like the Grinch who steals not only Christmas, but dang near every other day, too. These are what we call *toxic people* and they are to be avoided like the plague.

Others will tell you to reason with the person, try to kill them with kindness, etc. That's fine, but should those tactics fail to produce the desired results, other measures must be taken if you plan to not become toxic yourself. Birds of a feather, anyone?

The Victim: These people are very subtle with their toxicity. They tend to play the victim role whenever it's most convenient. According to them, bad things always happen to them and the world has a devised some elaborate conspiracy against their lives. Rarely do they take responsibility for their situations. It's always someone else's fault and they just happen to be the poor, unfortunate scapegoats. "Victims" are usually harmless and can typically be reasoned with if you bring the issue to their attention.

The One-Upper: These folks have a constant desire to outdo everything and everyone. You went to Hawaii for vacation, they suddenly decide to go to Fiji. You stayed in a four-star hotel. Guess what? They stayed in a 5-star hotel. You happened to meet Tom

Cruise on the beach. They claim to have met the Pope. "One-Uppers" delight in making others feel small by exhibiting how their lives are far superior. They tend to be quite pompous, but generally are more annoying than they are detrimental.

The Mudslinger: These malicious spirits are the worst of the bunch. They increase their egos by pulling others down and thrive on gossip and denigration. These meanies love to criticize, condemn, and judge anyone who has the misfortune of being within their line of sight. Loyalty is always an option with these people, as jealousy runs rampant with them. They often cannot be trusted and those who choose to associate with them must be on guard at all times.

During my research, I met a really fun gal named Giselle with a toxic "Mudslinger" story for the ages:

Giselle was happily engaged to her high school sweetheart, Aiden. She was a junior in college and he was a Marine, stationed roughly 1300 miles away. Despite their distance, he'd send her video messages and flowers every week. Sometimes he would go on trips with his battalion where he'd collect and send her little knickknacks from every stop he'd make.

Giselle's best friend, Beth, was in a relationship with a prison inmate who had been sentenced to a seven-year bid. At the time, he had only served one year.

Obviously, as her best friend, Giselle trusted Beth with everything. If Giselle was on the phone with Aiden and had to leave for a moment, she would allow Beth to talk to him until she returned. She assumed this sort of thing was okay.

One day, Beth called Giselle and indicated she needed to see her right away. When they connected, Beth handed Giselle a note that read, *Aiden wants to break up and would like all his belongings back. Don't call him now. He needs time to get over everything.*

With a look of horror and a feeling of utter confusion, I'm sure, Giselle asked Beth what the &#%! was going on. Beth stated she couldn't discuss it right then, that the breakup was for the best, and since Giselle was now single, she and Beth could hang out more without Aiden being "all in the way". Hmmm...

Of course, Giselle called Aiden anyway and demanded to know what this was all about. He revealed that Beth told him Giselle had been cheating on him with her biology lab partner for months!

Of course this entire story was a crock of bull Beth had concocted. (In fact, Giselle's lab partner was an out-and-proud gay man who she was positive had no interest in her, whatsoever.) When Giselle questioned Aiden about why he would believe such a thing, he stated that since Beth was Giselle's good friend, he *naïvely* assumed Beth wouldn't dare lie on Giselle—best friends don't do that, right?

What on earth made Beth decide she wanted to sabotage the blissful relationship her friend had? Jealousy and envy of Giselle's happiness, no doubt. It seems Beth was more than irritated with her jailbait boyfriend and the waiting game she had to play for him, so she fabricated some trumped-up charges against Giselle in order to force her into Beth's same miserable predicament. Mudslinging at it's finest.

(And yes, I *am* thinking what you're thinking. Why Beth assumed Giselle wasn't going to call her own boyfriend just because Beth told her not to is beyond me, as well.)

It's amazing how one person can affect so many other aspects of your being. A wise person once taught me we are but the average of the five people we spend the most time with. That's astounding! Eliminate the toxic people as soon as you can and watch your quality of life increase exponentially within a matter of days. Literally!

Like Giselle, I too found myself in a toxic relationship with someone. Once I eventually removed myself from this situation and subsequently surrounded myself with friends who loved me for who I was, and didn't try to change me to fit their predetermined mold, I was able to be comfortable in my own skin and just "do me".

✦Your T4 Action Plan✦

There are enough great friends out there that you can afford to spare a few bad seeds in order to preserve your own happiness.

The "victims" and the "one-uppers" may

be somewhat easy to handle, but those "mudslingers" are something else. The next time some green-eyed monster slithers over to deliver their crap in an attempt to steal your joy, tell 'em to keep on stepping. Negativity is contagious and **S.N.O.B.s** are naturally allergic.

Truth 5

"The Essence of A Woman Lies Not in the Clothes She Wears, But in the Decisions She Makes"

First impressions are of dire importance. Upon your first few meetings, please try to refrain from telling your love interest your entire life story. It's okay to hold back a bit at this point (how you stalked your last date for two weeks, how the past six guys in your life have hurt you, how you needed four therapists just to get over them, etc.) He'll think you're a headcase who's a glutton for punishment. There are even some guys who will attempt to take advantage of such situations by feeding their potential lady sweet nothings about how lame and moronic those other idiots were, how he'd never hurt her...blah blah blah. Then they use the poor girl's vulnerability to get whatever it is they really want (sex, money, status, etc.). You *know* it happens.

I have learned that if a man is truly into you, he will do whatever it takes to get to know you. If that means he has to drive three hours just to visit you every weekend, trust me, he will do it. Don't allow him to feed you empty promises and dreams of how he cares oh-so-much, and then tolerate it when he never spends time with you. If he very rarely calls or never calls, it means he's simply not interested. Point blank. There are few exceptions—his goldfish died and he's so devastated he can't cope with the tragic loss, he somehow ended up with lethal poison ivy and is in the hospital being treated...you get the idea. Do not waste your precious time and valuable energy hounding him like a stalker questioning why he has yet to return your calls. If he's not showing enough interest, believe me, he is replaceable. You are way too great of a catch to be bogged down by someone who talks the talk but walks the walk a bit too crookedly.

At the risk of sounding like some kind of lecturer, I've got to get this one off my chest, because it seems to be a truth that often gets ignored and too easily forgotten. There is a lot of power in what we have between our legs. Guys have literally gone insane trying to get the goods, which tells us our lovin' must be a lot more valuable than we often give it credit for. If we are attempting to form something beyond a sex-only arrangement with the men we are interested in, dues have got to be paid before they secure that highly-coveted access pass they crave so much. That means, if he isn't treating you with the respect, time, love, and honesty you require, don't waste your time *or* your body on him.

Similarly, I have found that sometimes

we ladies inadvertently feel pressured into sex. And that pressure doesn't always result from the persuasions of guys. Sometimes that influence we feel is self-inflicted.

"Our lovin' is a lot more valuable than we often give it credit for"

There was a period where my colleague, Shaina, had been single about two years and was ridiculously lonely. She began dating a couple of guys, one at a time, and consequently began sexual relationships with both of them (again, during different periods of time).

She divulged to me that, like most women, during these steamy sexual escapades, she felt more sexually liberated than ever before, although what she truly wanted was a relationship with each guy she was seeing during their respective times in her life. She felt amazingly free, sexy, and independent. However after each romp was over, Shaina soon reverted back to her depressed feelings of loneliness and isolation. Furthermore, this no-strings-attached casual sex made her feel nothing short of worthless, particularly because the desire to be in a relationship didn't seem to be reciprocated once the whole wham-bam-thank-you-ma'am was over. She indicated she often felt an intense need to be wanted by someone, and since it seemed as if she wasn't wanted by these men emotionally, physical servitude seemed to be the next best (temporary) fix.

I have to concur with Shaina. In my personal experience, attempting to fill an emotional void with sex is neither a vaccine nor a remedy for depressed feelings; it only serves to create and perpetuate them.

Now, I know I'm about to catch a lot of slack on this one, but hear me out. I understand every woman does not want to be married...but for those who do, consider **not** moving in with the boyfriend. Look at his from this perspective: what incentive is there to make that lifelong, legally-binding commitment if he's getting all the marital perks beforehand? He undoubtedly receives regular sex, home-cooked meals, a clean house, and everything else in exchange for what? Fixing a broken door handle every now and again? Please. Do not let him tell you that he just wants to "test drive the car before purchasing it". That's classic "I'm probably not going to marry you…ever" b.s.

Yes, I'm aware "shacking" (as my mother would call it) often turns into marriage, but I am also privy to the many, many women who are still waiting for that proposal decades after they started playing house. Most **S.N.O.B.s** require a bit more certainty when it comes to these kinds of things.

We all hear stories of women who ended up with twenty years of broken promises only to realize they're stuck in the dreaded "common-law wife zone".

Marriage, for those who desire it, may often be imitated, but never duplicated. Accept no semblances.

✦Your T5 Action Plan✦

Whatever it is you decide is best for you, be certain the decisions you make are totally of your own accord—without coercion and without guilt.

Your choices in these matters *have* to be contingent upon what *you* want, not what you feel you need to do in order to "keep" him or what you feel is what you "are supposed to do".

Pressure-free decision-making is both a right and a privilege. Feel free to exercise it at will.

"Love Is What Love Does"

Truths for Loving

Truth 6

"If It Walks Like a Duck and Talks Like a Duck, It Sure Ain't a Frog"

Sugarcoating sucks. I really loathe that kind of stuff. Just keep it 100% real with me, you know? Don't give me a bunch of cutesy reasons why something is the way it is. I want it straight, no chaser. So when I go to the bookstore, browse the relationship section, and see 500-page books with a bunch of fluff, I get a little concerned.

Do we really need 500 pages to tell us what's wrong and what's right about our relationships? Maybe some do. I beg to differ. While I know how complicated relationships can be, I also know we tend to create and incite much of that complexity ourselves.

Of course there are always ups and downs, but some things are simply unacceptable, so why waste the time with someone whose views are completely opposite and conflicting?

People tend to reevaluate their defining characteristics on their own terms, not because of constant complaining from their partners. It is impossible to successfully morph anyone's values, goals, or morals into our own personal models of perfection. Consider the following scenario:

"We create & incite much of the complexity in our relationships"

Carla meets Jake and decides he's someone she's really interested in. They begin dating. After the third date or so, he tells her he doesn't want kids. Never will. In fact, he's really irritated by them. Nothing is going to change his mind and he's never *ever* going to have any. Conversely, Carla totally adores children. Always will. In fact, she wants to raise a whole tribe of them. Like, yesterday. Nothing is going to change her mind. Both of these views are individually fine, but this is obviously not a match.

Why continue dating if their values and goals are so vastly opposite? This kind of thing is a deal breaker. We're not talking a "he loves Kung Pao Chicken and she hates Chinese food" kind of deal breaker, either.

But alas, they like one another so much that they continue dating and end up getting married. Five years down the road, Carla and her *Cheaper by the Dozen* complex go head-to-head with Jake's "No Kids" policy. They begin to resent each other because five years ago they already had this discussion, but chose to ignore it, thinking maybe they'd change each others' minds with their special "value-changing" superpowers.

Shaun, who volunteered to be one of the male guinea pigs during my research, was dating a woman he said "has abandonment and commitment issues". His reasoning for continuing the relationship: "I'm giving her the benefit of the doubt. I think she'll eventually see how nice of a guy I am and trust me completely."

It appeared as if the problems had been going on since before they even gave each other the boyfriend/girlfriend titles. Attempting to cultivate something with someone who has prior issues unrelated to him and thinking he's going to change her mind "because he's such a nice guy" probably wasn't the most fruitful journey to embark on. He complained about the incessant arguing and all the making up/breaking up they did, as he couldn't step one foot out the door without being constantly questioned about his whereabouts. It was driving him nuts. Shaun admitted his relationship was complicated, which actually sounded like a bit of an understatement.

Similarly, we always have to know the "why" of everything. For example, let's say your mate cheated. Does it really matter "why"? Sure, we can give excuses beyond excuses: "He doesn't pay enough attention to me", "She's always working", "He's too 'wham-bam' for me", "She's boring in bed". I find those excuses to be far from relevant. We're not slaves here – there's always the option to leave the relationship when dating. For those who are married, those vows still count and working through the issues "for better or for worse" is still a requirement. People don't get a pass to cheat just because they're unhappy their spouse refuses to do dishes on Thursdays.

As an "unmarried", I'd much rather my partner leave than cheat. Sure, it would hurt like hell, but at least have that level of respect for me. At the end of the day, I don't want to "talk it out". I don't need to know "why" you did it. As a cheater, you've lost my respect, and frankly, there's nothing more to discuss.

But some people are different and they need to know "the why". Enter the onslaught of the Sherlock Holmes game as they try to find out why their mate cheated, why they lied about something really big, why they did whatever unsavory deed—when in the end, it probably doesn't matter. Regardless of the reasoning, the person who has been cheated on is still mortified, terribly hurt, and might even be feeling a tad uncharacteristically vindictive. Getting over that painful feeling of betrayal usually takes a lot longer than had they sat down and discussed the underlying problem to begin with.

In my experience, when you accept such behaviors, it usually occurs again in some form or fashion at a later date because the silent message has been sent that "this is acceptable, and although I'm going to pester and nag you about it for what seems like eternity, I'll probably forgive you again because I love you *that* much. It doesn't matter that you don't love me enough to not do something you selfishly knew would bring me incredible hurt and pain."

You are worth so much more than that.

✦Your T6 Action Plan✦

Blinders are for horses, not humans. It's not the easiest thing in the world to accept things as they are, especially when those things involve the people we care for.

The concept of being an open-minded individual entails more than just being receptive to new ideas. It also means being able to see things as they are, and not for what we wish them to look like.

Don't develop new relationships based upon what you believe is someone's "potential" to be who you'd like them to be or what you'd like them to do. Focus on what the reality of the situation is, and whether or not you want to deal with what's there.

Life is too short, and equally too long, to spend it waiting on "what-if's" that you have no control over.

Yes, reality sometimes bites, but the truth will set us all free.

Truth 7

"The Romance Must Outshine the Rock"

Yours truly was once engaged to a man I wasn't the least bit interested in marrying. Yes, I know it sounds insanely stupid, but I really wanted to have a wedding. I mean, doesn't everyone? Most of us, at least? Come on…the white bedazzled gown, the friends and family, the three-tiered cake, a Savage Garden tribute band playing *I Knew I Loved You*, a deejay spinning Rick James and Earth Wind & Fire songs?

I was oh-so-ready and couldn't be more excited. Within 24 hours of him getting down on bended knee, I was happily wasting precious cell phone minutes to set up interviews with wedding planners and skipping company meetings to scour the internet for bridesmaids gowns. A week later, I had selected my colors, set up wedding and reception locations, and had finalized the guest list. I don't fool around, honey.

In retrospect, I was so pressed to be married because all my friends were getting hitched. Who wants to be that poor, lonely, last single friend?

Now, some may question why the heck I would engage in a relationship with someone I didn't even want to marry. I am now slightly embarrassed to say, I thought my sparkling personality might change him over time.

In my *naïveté,* I figured if I persevered just a little bit harder, something would click inside of him and he'd be who I needed him to be. That way, I could have my perfect wedding *and* my perfect marriage!

But the wedding was obviously the most important thing at the time. Later for the marriage. That's what marriage counselors are for, right? (Cut me some slack, I was young...kinda).

Much like myself, there are thousands, even millions of amazing women who are totally stoked about the idea of finally having "their day". We all want the frills, fluff, and French Riviera honeymoon. But are their current partners truly who they want to share those perks with?

Nobody's getting any younger, you know, and it often seems like everyone else is jumping the broom but us. Maybe the current flavor of the month is better than nothing?

I feel your pain. I mean, think about it: who wants to be "that girl"? The middle-aged, single chick stuck at home with her cats and *The Price is Right*? While that scenario may be acceptable to some, no one *actively* seeks out that lifestyle.

Yes, it would really suck to be "her". But wouldn't it suck even more royally to be married to someone who makes you cringe every time they want a little lovin'?

With that, I give you:

10 Ways to Tell if You're Marrying for the Rock Rather than the Romeo

1. You fantasize all the time about the wedding day, but living a life with him—eh, not so much.

2. You find lame excuses to prevent having to spend time with him ("Sorry, can't do dinner. Fido needs grooming, so I'm going to be brushing him *all* night.").

3. You are always on your period (interpretation: no booty for him!).

4. You get weirded out every time he mentions starting a family because you don't want to end up raising another "him".

5. You are totally irritated by his little nuances (when he cracks up at things that aren't that funny, when he rubs your leg in the movie theatre, when he purses his lips after eating teriyaki chicken).

6. You don't trust him to be good to you.

7. You sign a pre-nup not because you necessarily think it's a great idea, but because you know he's going to gank you for all your money when you finally get so annoyed with him, you decide to hit the road for good.

8. You long for the day you renew your vows just so you can be happy for the second time.

9. You plan on asking the reception deejay to play CeCe Peniston's *Keep On Walkin'* as a subliminal message. Maybe he'll get the hint.

10. You send him back to the jeweler

to upgrade that 2.5 carat diamond engagement ring to at least 5 carats. Marriage is supposed to be 50/50. If he's going to get what he wants, you need to get what you want.

✦Your T7 Action Plan✦

"Settling" is a cop out and desperation is not a good look. Recognize your worth and be assured that the confidence and beauty you radiate will attract the man you actually *want* to marry.

Because we don't want to (*gasp!*) be single, we often exert too much energy settling for people who aren't nearly ideal for us, and end up unknowingly missing the boats our true loves are riding on.

We all need someone who "gets" us, who understands who we are from the inside out. Someone who can appreciate our perhaps seemingly odd nuances (like how I tend to break out in song at the most random moments).

So, go for whoever it is and whatever it takes to generate *genuine* happiness for you. Because "good enough", frankly, isn't good enough.

Truth 8

"The Only Time A Woman Successfully Changes a Man is When He's in Diapers"

Maya Angelou once said, "If someone tells you who they are, believe them."

As women, we want to fix problems, make them perfect, mold them into what we want them to be. Because we are superwomen. And superwomen handle their business.

But if you think you can and will change your mate, you are in for a rude awakening. People, generally, do not change for other people. Instead, you will be viewed as a nag who he will eventually distance himself from.

Recall my example from Truth 7 where I assumed I could change my *fiancé* over time to make him a better mate for me (see page 84). The writings were on the wall from the beginning. They never said anything different, nor did they magically disappear. I just chose not to read them and decided I'd rewrite them to suit my needs, rather than take note of what was already there.

Attempting to change someone is like betting your life savings on a team that hasn't won a game all season. They more than likely will not win and you're pretty much guaranteed to lose all your money, but you hope like hell they'll pull through this time, despite their 0-14 record. What, with all our other obligations to work, school, family, and life, no one has time to commit to yet another "project" that will surely yield frustrating results at best.

While pregnant with her boyfriend's child, Meghan was interviewed for an unrelated focus group project where she discussed how after sixteen years of dating this guy, he was just learning to love her properly. She was thrilled that he finally decided to be monogamous, that he wanted to be totally honest with her. She stated she put forth a lot of effort during each and every one of those sixteen years in order to turn him into her Mr. Perfect.

"If someone tells you who they are, believe them"

Hold up. Wait a minute... Sixteen years and the guy was *just* figuring out how to love her the way she needed to be loved? This had to be some sort of joke. I had to get a hold of this woman.

Meghan and I met and discussed this situation. Even she knew how nutty it sounded. *Sixteen years??* Do you have any idea how many better ways I can find to spend sixteen years of my life? Sheesh!

I was willing to bet that if the guy hadn't learned how to love her in sixteen years, he was never going to learn. He seemed to know she wasn't going anywhere. Every time she'd threaten to leave him, she'd give him that "one last chance" we all know too well. According to her, one last chance had turned into about thirty last chances. That's over two last chances a year!

About four months after the project ended, Meghan informed me that her guy's monogamy took a back seat, yet again. Like I said, people, generally, do not change for other people.

✦Your T8 Action Plan✦

Here's your new goal: stop trying to change folks. Like, today. Seriously. They don't change. They rarely ever will. They will be who are they are and either we accept them or we press on. Bada-bing, bada-boom.

Now, there are some things you can work on, should you desire to do so.

Let's say he's a fantastic person and a great guy to you, but he can't dance worth a lick. If you have the burning desire to fix his two left feet, by all means, knock yourself out.

What I'm referring to are personality traits. Those things do not change, for those traits are what make us who we are, yes? If you **can't** handle who he is, find someone else who you **can** accept. Otherwise you will end up feeling defeated because of how tired you are from nagging and trying to change the guy, only for him to become resistant and onery. Wouldn't you become pretty irritated if somebody was constantly trying to change *you*?

It might be possible for people to change what they do, but it's nearly impossible for them to change who they are—unless those people make the very personal decision to change for themselves.

Truth 9

"You Don't Have to Catch a Beat-Down to Feel the Pain"

It's time to get a little serious. Anyone who has been in a controlling relationship with a partner has more than likely been a victim of emotional abuse.

Many people don't realize they are being jerked around in emotionally abusive relationships because it's such a silent and subtle form of abuse. In fact, many outside of the mental health community don't even recognize it as abuse. But those who have experienced it will beg to differ, without a doubt.

Emotional abuse is so cleverly discreet that the victim may be willing to accept it, assuming that the way it manifests is simply an unavoidable part of their partner's personality. It's what makes them who they are, right?

Well, yes and no. It may be a part of their personality, but that doesn't mean anyone should have to deal with such treatment. There's nothing worse than losing yourself in an attempt to make someone happy for whom nothing is ever good enough.

You know you might be a victim of emotional abuse if your partner:

- Forces you to choose between them and someone or something important in your life
- Tells you that you are overly sensitive and seems to become even meaner when you cry
- Punches holes in walls, breaks objects, throws things across the room, or otherwise displays violence when angry

- Frequently says things one way then later denies it or makes you feel as if you misunderstood them
- Acts immature, vengeful, selfish, or mean, then accuses you of those actions
- Accuses you of lying when you've never lied to them
- Accuses you of cheating when you've never cheated on them or given them reason to think you've cheated
- Is ridiculously insecure
- Tells you they support your endeavors but does everything to stand in the way of making them a reality
- Attempts to occupy all your free time
- Gives you a hard time about going out without them
- "Stalks" you on social networking

sites (e.g., MySpace, Facebook, etc.) and keeps track of your virtual wall messages and/or number of "friends" on these sites

- Manipulates you with constant contradictions and lies, then makes you feel as if your memory is poor when you bring up something they've stated before
- Has ever purposely and maliciously left you stranded somewhere
- Vows to change after you attempt to break up with them, then goes right back to their same tactics after a period of time
- Makes you feel as if everything is your fault
- Makes you feel trapped and afraid of them
- Forces you to lie to them about things that shouldn't have to be lied about (e.g., hanging with friends, going to see your family, going out

of town for a girls' weekend) just so they won't give you a hard time about it

- Habitually leaves you at home alone while they go out and hang with their friends
- Is extremely secretive and/or gets mad if you ask them "too many" questions
- Causes you to look forward to going to work as a temporary escape from them
- Causes you to find yourself crying constantly and longing for the more compassionate side of them

It's quite clear how much of a miserably stressful situation this is for the victim.

Now, to be fair, actions do speak a heck of a lot louder than words. If you're telling your man, "You're my one and only", yet you spend little, if any, time with him, he's bound to take your words with a grain of salt and likely act out a bit in hopes of getting some much needed attention from you.

But, let's argue for a moment that you *are* showing him through your actions, doing everything in your power to let him know he's your end all, be all. I will personally attest that no amount of action will satisfy an insecure mate.

In order for any relationship to be successful, both parties must be secure within themselves, first and foremost. Otherwise, subtle, as well as extravagant actions, gifts, time spent, etc. will be a complete and utter waste of time on the parts of one or both parties.

As women, we are classic caregivers. Generally, we desire to nurture and please those around us. When it is established that we aren't doing so, we attempt to find bigger and better ways of pleasing.

A controlling partner will constantly take advantage of the situation, driving their mates crazy from simply trying to make things right.

More signs of emotional abuse:

- Ignoring your feelings but making certain theirs are known
- Disrespecting, humiliating and/or yelling at you in public or in front of others
- Demeaning your family traditions, religious beliefs, or other things of importance to you
- Being constantly sarcastic to the point where it becomes hurtful, then telling you it's only a joke and that you should lighten up
- Attempting to isolate you from your friends and family or giving you a hard time about spending time with your friends and family
- Complaining about you constantly but rarely having anything good to say about you, with the "good"

things sounding generic (e.g., you're kind, you're pretty) as opposed to the complaints which are very detailed and explicit

It's a vicious cycle. The abuser hurts their partner, who knows it's wrong and tells the abuser they refuse to take such treatment. The abuser apologizes and does everything in their power to win their partner back. Eventually, the abused partner gives in and provides the abuser the opportunity to rectify the situation. This repeats and repeats and eventually the abused partner is stuck in a rut of a cycle they can't get out of. They love their mates so much that they just know "this time" the emotional abuse will cease. Only it ceases for a few weeks, maybe a few months, then it's right back to square one.

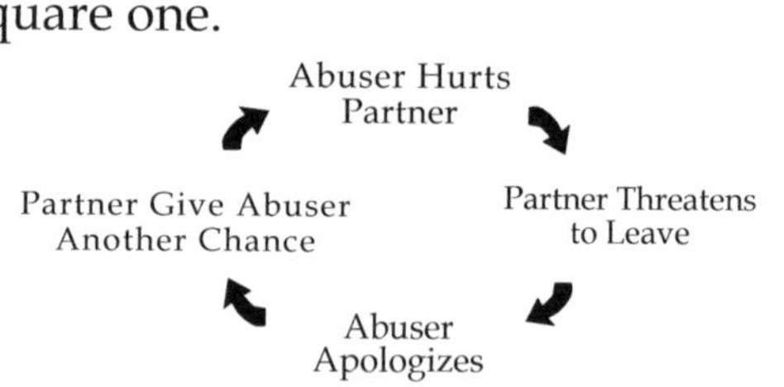

✦Your T9 Action Plan✦

We all have to take responsibility for our actions and be honest with ourselves. If you're not treating your guy right or if you are emasculating him, you probably know it. If you're good on your end, you probably know that, too. So, it's fairly easy to assess whether someone is simply asking to be loved properly or if they are being emotionally abusive. If the issue appears to be the latter, it's time to throw that dude a peace sign and get the hell out of Dodge. Because, as we know, personality traits, for the most part, do not change.

And **S.N.O.B.s** don't go for that mess anyway.

 Afterword

Congratulations, girlfriend! You are now a complete and utter **S.N.O.B.** Just who *do* you think you are?

Now that you've begun learning to tap into the entirely beautiful woman you are, remember to not fall back into any old self-*un*loving habits.

One of the most vital truths my mother ever taught me was that we only have one life to live, and guess what? This is it!

We don't have time to dwell in past situations or on past people who we have removed ourselves from for good reason.

Yesterday is history, tomorrow is a

mystery. And we all know the Wayback Machine doesn't exist. Push forward and be open to the blessings to come, 'cause, baby, you are about to get showered with them!

You're loving yourself completely, doing what's best for you, and becoming emotionally self-reliant. I guarantee love will be a heck of a lot easier to deal with.

You don't have to go on some elaborate mission in pursuit of "the one". Entirely beautiful women radiate and attract "the one" effortlessly and in due time. Patience is a virtue. Handle what you can control (yourself) and the rest will fall into place.

Of course, you have to go out and meet men. No random guy is going to just come a'knocking at your front door. At least, let's hope not. That would be odd and, quite frankly, scary.

Efforts must be made, however the arguing and fighting will immediately cease because you aren't trying to mold anyone's personality to be conducive to your liking. You are focused on you and that's awesome! You're rolling with the punches, and this time, not getting knocked out for the count.

When we begin to focus on how to make ourselves better people and fall in love with ourselves 100% from the inside out, it seems as if exterior happiness just effortlessly materializes. And we discover that pain and love are most definitely not one in the same.

It is a beautiful thing when someone who cares about you and wants to make you happy enters your world. Someone who wants only you, who wants to show you they are appreciative of you, and who adores the royalty you are.

A **S.N.O.B.** wouldn't settle for anything less.

"Get Your Mind Right"

Appendices

Appendix I

Truths At-a-Glance

Truths for Living
"You Stand Alone"

Truth 1
"Beauty Doesn't Fade, Elasticity Does"

Truth 2
"Grown-Ups Don't Come With Manuals, Either"

Truth 3
"A Good Hussy Makes a Poor Housewife"

Truth 4
"Negativity is to Life as Dog Poo is to Shoes: Once You Step In It, It's Hard as Heck to Get Off"

Truth 5
"The Essence of a Woman Lies Not in the Clothes She Wears, But in the Decisions She Makes"

Truths for Loving
"Love is What Love Does"

Truth 6

"If It Walks Like a Duck and Talks Like a Duck, It Sure Ain't a Frog"

Truth 7

"The Romance Must Outshine the Rock"

Truth 8

"The Only Time a Woman Successfully Changes a Man is When He's in Diapers"

Truth 9

"You Don't Have to Catch a Beat-Down to Feel the Pain"

Appendix II

Tips for S.N.O.B.s

1. Do not attempt to hurt your ex by sleeping with his friend(s) in retaliation for any pain he has caused you. This will be completely counterproductive and you'll likely end up with a severely dreadful reputation that will haunt you for years to come.

2. Never compromise your integrity, morals, or values for anyone.

3. No relationship is worth tears of pain and when you find one that is, it won't cause you to cry.

4. Believe in the miracle of *you*.

5. Get a life. Your existence should not revolve around your mate's world. Have your own friends, career, dreams, and aspirations. Be interesting on your own.

6. Either accept him or leave. Do not waste your energy trying to change your partner. Your efforts will be fruitless.

7. Never accept a cheater, an abuser, or a disrespectful lover. There are too many fish in the sea for that drama.

8. Pain and love are mutually exclusive entities. One exists totally and completely without the other.

9. Never revisit a situation that isn't healthy for you.

10. Refuse to live your life in rewind, "one more chances", and "what-if's".

Appendix III

Food for Thought

We ask ourselves, "Who am I to be brilliant, gorgeous, talented, fabulous?" Actually, who are you not to be? You are a child of God. Your playing small does not serve the world. There is nothing enlightened about shrinking so that other people won't feel insecure around you. We are all meant to shine, as children do.

~Marianne Williamson

Dream big or you might not ever get beyond your front yard.

~Anonymous

Don't make someone your priority when you're only an option to them. Your time is limited, so don't waste it living someone else's life. Don't be trapped by dogma, which is living with the results of other peoples' thinking. Don't let the noise of others' opinions drown out your own inner voice. And most importantly, have the courage to follow your heart and intuition. They somehow already know what you truly want to become.

~Steve Jobs

Whether you think you can or you can't, you are right.

~Henry Ford

You may say, "But I am only human." This is the understatement of your life. You are not "only" human – you are also divine potential.

~ Eric Butterworth

True discovery consists not in finding new landscapes, but in seeing the same landscape with new eyes.

~ Marcel Proust

No one can make you feel inferior without your consent.

~Eleanor Roosevelt

Appendix IV

Resources for S.N.O.B.s

Contact Me

- Visit the blog & the website – **www.TheDuckWalk.com**
- Email me – **gwen@theduckwalk.com**

Mental Health America

www.nmha.org

2000 N. Beauregard Street, 6th Floor
Alexandria, VA 22311
Phone (703) 684-7722
Fax (703) 684-5968
Toll free (800) 969-6642
TTY Line 800/433-5959

Mental Health America (formerly known as the National Mental Health Association) is the country's leading nonprofit dedicated to helping ALL people live mentally healthier lives. With more than 320 affiliates nationwide, Mental Health America represents a growing movement of Americans who promote mental wellness for the health and well-being of the nation—everyday and in times of crisis.

National Association for Self-Esteem (NASE)

www.self-esteem-nase.org

The purpose of NASE is to fully integrate self-esteem into the fabric of American society so that every individual, no matter what their age or background, experiences personal worth and happiness.

NASE strives to promote awareness of self-esteem, as well as provide vision, leadership, and advocacy for improving the human condition through the enhancement of healthy self-esteem.

NASE believes self-esteem is "the experience of being capable of meeting life's challenges and being worthy of happiness". The organization also believes in and encourages personal responsibility and accountability.

U.S. Dept. of Health & Human Services

Mental Health Services Locator

http://mentalhealth.samhsa.gov/databases

This tool provides comprehensive information concerning mental health services and resources based upon your geographic location.

Building Self-Esteem Help Guide

http://mentalhealth.samhsa.gov/publications/allpubs/sma-3715/default.asp

This online guide offers information on what self-esteem is, as well as helpful activities to assist you in increasing yours. It also offers insight on how to change your negative thoughts into positive ones and teaches you how to remove depression from your life.

Notes

Notes

Notes

Notes

About Gwen

Growing up, perhaps Gwen Jimmere had a childhood and family life that's becoming less and less typical in American households nowadays—she actually lived the proverbial happy childhood at home with two parents, a sister and a dog who all loved her dearly. As a matter of fact, Gwen especially credits her mother with teaching her everything she knows now about intimate relationships—and she doesn't get tired of saying she should have listened to her mom all along.

Now, this award-winning filmmaker is a woman on a mission—and her mission is to help young women like herself see the reason to honestly take the measure of the people they invite into their lives, and to show her readers how to spot the bad seeds in the bunch and get rid of them for good!

Gwen's career moves have taken her on a tour of industries that are all about communicating to large audiences—she's been a television producer, a film director, a stage manager for theatre, a book editor, a writer for magazines, music, and movies, and has even owned a very successful online magazine.

Having lived through her fair share of extreme heartbreaks and all of the consequences that follow, Gwen has become a staunch advocate for emotional abuse awareness and self-esteem in women. Knowing that Gwen is a member of Mental Health America (formerly the National Mental Health Association) and the National Association for Self-Esteem makes perfect sense. This "good girl" grew up to make the same kinds of bad decisions so many young women make, and has lived to tell the tale and offer a way out, as well as a hand to those who can profit by what she's learned.

Gwen is here to relay that wise advice, help people stop lying to themselves about their relationships, learn to be accountable for the decisions they make, and move on to their real chances for happy lives with partners who'll love and respect them for the royalty they are.

Made in the USA